RESEARCHING
COPYRIGHT RENEWAL

RESEARCHING COPYRIGHT RENEWAL
A Guide To Information And Procedure

Iris J. Wildman
M.L.S., J.D.

Rhonda Carlson
M.L.S., J.D.

Fred B. Rothman & Co.
Littleton, Colorado

1989

Library of Congress Cataloging-in-Publication Data
Wildman, Iris J.
　Researching copyright renewal : a guide to information and procedure / by Iris J. Wildman and Rhonda Carlson.
　　p.　cm.
　Includes bibliographical references.
　ISBN 0-8377-1352-8 (alk. paper)
　1. Library of Congress. Copyright Office. Catalog of copyright entries.　2. Copyright--Duration--United States--Research--Methodology.　3. Copyright cataloging--United States.　I. Carlson, Rhonda.　II. Title.
Z642.W53　1989
018'1--dc20　　　　　　　　　　　　　　　　　　　　　89-78539
　　　　　　　　　　　　　　　　　　　　　　　　　　　　CIP

© 1989 by Fred B. Rothman & Co.
All rights reserved.

Printed in the United States of America

To the memory of

Stella Wildman, Meira G. Pimsleur and Fred B. Rothman

for their faith

To

Edward J. Gac

for his faith

and to

"Puffer" and the late "Lord Byron"

for their patience

TABLE OF CONTENTS

Preface	ix
Part I: Summary of Copyright and Renewal	
Chapter 1	3
Copyright in Brief	3
Publication	4
Notice	6
Duration and Renewal	7
Chapter 2	11
Copyright Renewal Investigation Procedure	11
Summary of Procedure	17
Part II: Using the *Catalog of Copyright Entries*	
Sample Entry in the *Catalog of Copyright Entries*	23
List of Abbreviations: Copyright Claim Bases	25
List of Abbreviations: Other Abbreviations	27
Catalog of Copyright Entries Volumes to Check: By Year (Date Chart)	31
Year-by-Year Analysis	
1941	33
1942	34
1943	35
1944	36
1945	37
1946	38
1947	39
1948	40
1949	41
1950	42
1951	43
1952	45
1953	46

Year-by-Year Analysis (*continued*)

1954	47
1955	48
1956	49
1957	50
1958	51
1959	52
1960	53
1961	54
1962	55
1963	56
1964	57
1965	58
1966	59
1967	60
1968	61
1969	62
1970	63
1971	64
1972	65
1973	66
1974	68
1975	69
1976	70
1977	71
1978	72
1979	73
1980	74
1981	75
Footnotes	77
Selected Basic Resources	81
Index	83

PREFACE

We have been involved in publishing reprints of titles for which copyright has expired and thus have been investigating copyright renewals for some time. The U.S. Copyright Office has been inconsistent in its format for listing copyright renewals in the *Catalog of Copyright Entries* (originally spelled *Catalogue* until 1934 when the spelling changed to *Catalog*). Each time we have used the *Catalog*, we had to search our memories on how to use each different year so as not to miss entries due to misunderstanding the format of that particular year.

As we compared notes we had made on using the *Catalog*, we decided to pool our information and our efforts and share this knowledge with others who also may wish to investigate the status of copyright. Though the U.S. Copyright Office has circulars on copyright renewal and the investigative process, these circulars do not describe the format and the anomalies of the *Catalog*.

Other than a brief explanation of copyright in general, this publication extends only to information on investigating the status of copyright renewals of books and pamphlets, and omits any discussion of renewal rights, assignments, or transfers. The rationale for renewal and for the changes in duration can be found in some of the treatise materials and the legislative history of the Copyright Act of 1976, as noted in the "Selected Basic Resources" on page 81.

We would like to express our appreciation and thanks to Professor Paul Goldstein, Stanford Law School, an expert in copyright law; to W. David Rozkuszka, Foreign and International Documents Librarian, Jonsson Library of Government Documents, Stanford University Libraries; to Mary Wilder, Public Services Librarian, University of Denver School of Law Library and former Government Documents Librarian and Professor of Government Documents; and to Sheila Jarrett, Editorial/Production Manager, Fred B. Rothman & Co., for reading and making suggestions on the manuscript.

Rhonda Carlson
Iris J. Wildman
December 1989

PART I

SUMMARY OF COPYRIGHT AND RENEWAL

CHAPTER 1

COPYRIGHT IN BRIEF

In order to understand copyright renewal, it is important to understand what copyright is, what it does, and how long it endures. Therefore, a brief discussion of copyright basics is necessary.

Copyright is a form of protection provided by law to authors of original works in literature, drama, music, art, and certain other intellectual works. It is provided for by the Constitution of the United States of America in Article I, section 8, clause 8, which in enumerating the powers of Congress, states: "To promote the Progress of Science and useful Arts, by securing for limited Times to Authors and Inventors the exclusive Right to their respective Writings and Discoveries." It is statutorily provided for by Public Law 94-553, October 19, 1976, effective January 1, 1978, Title 17, *United States Code (U.S.C.)*, known as the Copyright Act of 1976. This protection extends to both published and unpublished works.[1] Under Section 106,[2] the owner of the copyright, not the owner/possessor of a book, manuscript, painting, etc.,[3] has the exclusive right to produce and to authorize reproductions of a work, prepare derivation, distribute copies, and perform or display the copyrighted work publicly.

It is illegal for anyone to violate these rights granted to the owner of copyright. However, there are limitations on the exclusive rights of copyright as provided in Sections 107-119,[4] such as the limitations which refer to fair use to reproduce copy for criticism, teaching, research, comment, or news reporting in Section 107, or for a library or archives to reproduce more than one copy of a work without purposes of marketing, where their collections are open to the public or researchers and the copy includes a notice of copyright in Section 108. For those who wonder about photocopying by library users, the law states that libraries and archives are not liable for the "unsupervised use of reproducing equipment located on its premises: Provided, That such equipment displays a notice that the making of a copy may be subject to the copyright law...."[5]

Factors to be considered in fair use under Section 107[6] include:

1) the purpose and character of the use, including whether such use is of a commercial nature or is for nonprofit educational purposes;
2) the nature of the copyrighted work;
3) the amount and substantiality of the portion used in relation to the copyrighted work as a whole;
4) the effect of the use upon the potential market for or value of the copyrighted work.

Once a publication is in the public domain, meaning open to anyone to copy, reproduce, or market, its copyright protection is lost and the exclusive rights, such as fair use and reproduction, no longer apply.[7]

PUBLICATION

Only the author/creator or those to whom the copyright is assigned can claim copyright. In the case of an employee preparing work within the scope of employment, the copyright belongs to the employer as defined under "work made for hire."[8]

In order to secure copyright under the Copyright Act of 1909, it was required that a work was either published with the copyright notice or was registered in the Copyright Office. This requirement has been changed under the Copyright Act of 1976. Section 102(a)[9] states that copyright protection extends to "original works of authorship fixed in any tangible medium of expression, now known or later developed, from which they can be perceived, reproduced or otherwise communicated, either directly or with the aid of a machine or device...." However, Section 102(b)[10] states that copyright protection for an original work of authorship does not extend "to any idea, procedure, process, system, method of operation, concept, principle, or discovery, regardless of the form in which it is described, explained, illustrated, or embodied in such work."

Copyright protection does not extend to any work of the United States government,[11] that is, materials published by the U.S. Government Printing Office and by agencies of the United States Government are in the public domain. However, the United States Government can receive and hold copyrights transferred to it under Section 105. Also works commissioned by the United States Government can be copyrighted.

The official court reports or opinions, and the laws or statutes of the U.S. Government and the states of the United States are in the public domain. If such reports and statutes contain annotations or other editorial input by reporters, editors or commercial publishers, that editorial material is subject to copyright, such as the compilation by the reporter for the Alabama Reports noted in the illustration for 1953 on page 46, or the headnotes or annotations in the West Publishing Company or the Lawyers Co-Operative Publishing Company editions of the *U.S. Reports* or the *United States Code*.

> The courts of this country have long held that neither judicial opinions nor statutes can be copyrighted. See *Wheaton v. Peters*, 33 U.S. 599 (8 Peters) (1834); *Howell v. Miller*, 91 F. 129 (6th Cir. 1898); *Davidson v. Wheelock*, 27 F. 61 (C.C.D. Minn. 1866). The rationale of this rule is set forth in *Building Officials and Code Administration v. Code Technology, Inc.*, 628 F.2d 730, 734 (1st Cir. 1980)....[12]

Justice Harlan said in *Howell v. Miller*:

> It was suggested in argument that no one can obtain the exclusive right to publish the laws of a state in a book prepared by him. This general proposition cannot be doubted. And it may also be said that any person desiring to publish the statutes of a state may use any copy of such statutes to be found in any printed book, whether such book is the property of the state or the property of an individual.[13]

NOTICE

In order for the public to know if a work was protected by copyright, under the Copyright Acts of 1909 and 1976, it was required that a publication show a notice of copyright and the name of the copyright owner on copies or phonorecords that were publicly distributed under the authority of the copyright owner. This copyright notice could be used by the copyright owner without permission from or registration with the Copyright Office. However, under the Berne Convention Implementation Act of 1988, effective March 1, 1989, Section 7(a)(2), notice has been made optional by changing the wording "shall be placed on all" to "may be placed on" in 17 U.S.C. Section 401(a).[14]

According to the 1976 Act for Section 401(b), now amended by the Berne Amendments, Section 7(a)(3), "If a notice appears on the copies, it"[15] shall consist of three elements for "visually perceptible copies" (excluding phonorecords of sound recordings):[16]

1) The letter C in a circle, ©, or the word "Copyright" or the abbreviation "Copr;"
2) The year of first publication of the work; and
3) The name of the copyright owner of the work.[17]

An example of the three elements together is usually found on the verso of the title page of books or monographs, or at the bottom of the first page of periodical articles if the copyright is owned by the writer, e.g.,

© 1988 Fred B. Rothman & Co.

The position of notice is authorized by Section 401(c)[18] and the regulations concerning the form and position are found in the *Code of Federal Regulations (C.F.R.)*.[19]

DURATION AND RENEWAL

Under the Copyright Act of 1976, effective January 1, 1978,[20] works that are created on or after the effective date are automatically protected by copyright where the works are fixed in a tangible medium of expression, and are within the subject matter of copyright as stated in Sections 102 and 103,[21] whether published or unpublished.[22] The copyright owner has the exclusive right to do and to authorize reproductions, prepare derivative works, distribute copies to the public, or display or perform the work publicly as noted earlier in Section 106.[23] The copyright protection endures for a term consisting of the author's life plus 50 years.[24] In the case of joint authors, the duration endures as long as the last surviving author's life plus 50 years.[25] If the work is a "work made for hire," the duration is 75 years from the time of publication, or 100 years from its creation, whichever expires first.[26] For example, a work created in 1980, but not published until 2010, would expire in 2080, not 2085, 100 years from the time of creation. Section 303,[27] which discusses works created but not published or copyrighted before January 1, 1978, allows for copyright to begin January 1, 1978 and endure for the author's life plus 50 years and in no case to expire prior to December 31, 2002, and if published on or before December 31, 2002, to endure to December 31, 2027.

With the change to the author's life plus 50 years, there is no renewal process for works copyrighted after December 31, 1977. Since works are copyrighted through the calendar year under the Copyright Act of 1976,[28] works will expire on December 31st of the 50th year after the death of the author.

However, renewal was a protection extended under the Copyright Act of 1909, and it is this process with which we are concerned in this publication.

Under the Copyright Act of 1909, works were copyrighted for a period of 28 years with the option of a renewal term for an additional 28 years, making a total of 56 years of copyright protection. Copyrighted works were eligible for renewal during the 28th year of their first term. However, it should be noted that there can be no renewal unless a work has been registered for its first term. Renewal is not automatic. It was required that the renewal application and fee be received by the Copyright Office during the 28th year, the renewal period, and before the renewal deadline which was the anniversary date of the 28th year, for the renewal to be effective. When the new Copyright Act became effective on January 1, 1978, new rules for renewal also became effective. One of the new rules extends the copyright term to the end of the calendar year in which the copyright otherwise would have expired[29] rather than on the exact anniversary date as under the old Act.

There are several time periods for copyright that are affected by the new Act. Works that were copyrighted before 1950 which had been renewed and were in their second term between December 31, 1976 and December 31, 1977, inclusive, were automatically extended to last for a total term of 75 years from the end of the year in which the copyright was originally secured.[30] Thus the renewal term became 47 years instead of 28, as noted above. *If renewed*, only the extension of the renewal period from 28 years to 47 years is automatic. For example, a work that was originally copyrighted on May 10, 1921 and renewed between May 10, 1948 and May 10, 1949, its 28th year, would have expired on May 10, 1977 under the old Act. The new Act automatically extends the second term to 47 years or a total of 75 years, with the expiration date of December 31, 1996, not May 10, 1996.

Works that were renewed between December 31, 1976 and December 31, 1977 also were granted the automatic extension of 47 years, even though their second term would not have begun until sometime in 1978.[31]

Beginning in 1962 there were a series of congressional acts,[32] the first of which was effective September 19, 1962, which continually extended copyrights that were in their second term until the new law took effect, thus extending their second term for 47 years or a total of 75 years from the original date of copyright. For example:

> A work that was first entered for copyright on October 5, 1907 and renewed in 1935, would formerly have fallen into the public domain after October 5, 1963. The first Act extended the copyright to December 31, 1965; the second Act extended it to December 31, 1967; the third Act extended it to December 31, 1968; the fourth Act extended it to December 31, 1969; the fifth Act extended it to December 31, 1970; the sixth Act extended it to December 31, 1971; the seventh Act extended it to December 31,

1972; the eighth Act extended it to December 31, 1974; the ninth Act extended it to December 31, 1976, and the Copyright Act of 1976 finally extended the copyright through the end of 1982 (75 years from the end of the year in which the copyright was originally secured).[33]

Any work for which the copyright renewal expired prior to September 19, 1962, was not extended, and therefore, entered the public domain.

There are copyrights that were in their first term on January 1, 1978 when the new law took effect. These still must be renewed within *strict time limits,* otherwise they will lose copyright protection and enter the public domain at the end of their 28th year. These time limits are due to the new rule which changed the expiration of copyrights from the anniversary date in the 28th year to the end of the 28th calendar year. As before, renewal can be made only during the 28th year, but that is now a calendar year, not the anniversary date, that is, from December 31 of the 27th year through December 31 of the following or 28th year. Renewal will extend these copyrights for an additional 47 years or 75 years from the original date of copyright. However, if not renewed, the copyright will be lost and cannot be restored.

Works that were copyrighted prior to 1978 and were not renewed retain copyright for the original 28 years only, after which they enter the public domain.

Nothing in the law of 1909 states whether renewal had to be shown on copies of a work issued during the renewal period. Many works still in copyright due to renewal may be out-of-print, but are, nevertheless, still protected by copyright. "Out-of-print' and "out-of-copyright" are two different concepts and should not be confused.

CHAPTER 2

COPYRIGHT RENEWAL INVESTIGATION PROCEDURE

The problem in determining whether a copyright has been renewed and when it expires is not only in interpreting the law, but in determining how to find a renewal by using the appropriate tools. The purpose of this book is to lead you through the renewal investigation process, and explain the variations in the *Catalog of Copyright Entries*.

The Copyright Office *Catalog of Copyright Entries*, for which publication is authorized under Section 707(a),[34] lists all the types of materials, that is, books, pamphlets, music, maps, serials, etc., by author or other main heading, and title, for which copyright was applied for and granted.

However, neither publication nor registration is required to secure copyright under the 1976 Act since copyright is automatically secured when the work is created, that is, it is fixed in such as a copy or phonorecord for the first time.[35] But under the Copyright Act of 1909, in effect through December 31, 1977, a work published without a notice of copyright or compliance with other requirements of the law would be considered in the public domain. To determine if a work has been copyrighted, the *Catalog* can be checked for the year of publication or the succeeding year. The copyright registration information is entered under the name of the copyright owner such as the author. Unless it is a "work made for hire," the entry is most often found under the author. If the work does not show a distinct author, other elements such as publisher, association, or institution can be searched. There are usually some references in either the current registrations, renewals, or the index (the place has changed through the years) to lead from the entry not used to the correct copyright entry. For example, in the *Catalog* for 1940, in the case of a woman's maiden name used as author, but where the registration is under the married name, the index shows the cross reference as follows:

> Allen (Gracie) See Burns, (G.A.)

Under Burns (G.A.) in the index, the entry number 9402 is given. Under that number in the registration list is found the following:

> [Burns, Gracie Allen]* Beverly Hills, Calif.
> How to become president, by Gracie Allen. Illustrated by Charles Lofgren. © June 21, 1940; A144721.
> 9402

As stated above, renewal must be applied for and obtained during the 28th year of publication, otherwise the copyright is terminated. Therefore, prior to 1978 when copyrights still expired on the anniversary date of the original copyright, renewals are listed in the *Catalog* either in the 27th, 28th, or 29th year, depending on the date when the renewal was granted and the information published. For example:

> A work that was originally copyrighted on May 10, 1940 had to be renewed during its 28th year which was May 10, 1967 to May 10, 1968, the date on which it would expire without renewal. Therefore, the renewal information could show up in the *Catalog* for 1967, the beginning of the 28th anniversary year, or 1968, or even 1969 if the work had been published late in the year, such as December rather than May. Consequently, the search for renewals involves the use of the *Catalog* for the 27th and 28th years, and possibly the 29th and even the 30th year if not found in the earlier years, particularly if the copyright expiration is toward the end of the calendar year.

But how does one know if a book was copyrighted? First, as noted in Chapter 1, a notice of copyright had to appear on the work, usually on the verso of the title page, showing the copyright symbol, date, and copyright owner. Assuming a work was copyrighted in 1940, the copyright entry then would appear in the 1940 *Catalog* such as the Burns entry on page 12. The Burns renewal was made in 1968, its 28th year, as follows:

>BURNS, GRACIE ALLEN.
>   How to become President, by Gracie
>   Allen. Illustrated by Charles
>   Lofgren. © 21Jun40; A144721;
>   George N. Burns (Wr); 6Mar68;
>   R431073.

The renewal entry shows the author, title, illustrator, copyright date (©), registration number ("A" number), the claimant (Wr), the renewal date and the renewal registration ("R" number). (An illustration of the elements of a copyright registration entry appears on page 23 and the "List of Abbreviations: Copyright Claim Bases" appears on page 25.)

At the time of renewal, expiration would have been on the anniversary date. But as stated previously, under the 1976 Act, all expirations have been extended to December 31 of the anniversary year.[36] Because this publication was renewed, it will expire on December 31, 2015, 75 years from the original date of copyright in 1940.

If a work does not show a copyright notice, but only a publication date, it can be checked in the *Catalog* for copyright in the year of publication and possibly the succeeding year. Copyright under the 1909 Act was generally obtained by publication and notice of copyright.[37] Works prior to 1978, without a notice of copyright, that are not found in the *Catalog*, may be in the public domain. If still in doubt after doing all of the search oneself, then the records of the Copyright Office should be checked as noted in "A Note of Caution" on page 18.

Early in the twentieth century, renewals were listed month by month at the end of each issue of the *Catalog's* "Pamphlet" issue. The index noted which copyright registration number the renewal followed.

Through the 1945 *Catalog*, there was one combined index for current registrations and renewals. In 1946, copyright information was appended to the current registration using the form of the Library of Congress main entry card, and adding the date of copyright, the copyright owner, and the copyright registration number, as follows:

> [Norway, Nevil Shute] 1899-
> >Vinland the good, by Nevil Shute [pseud.]
>
> [New York] W. Morrow & co., inc., c1946.
> >126 p. 22 cm.
> >Map on lining papers.
> >Drama.
> >© 2Oct46; 2c 19Sep46; William Morrow & co., inc.; A 6770.

The renewals were alphabetically arranged in a separate section, following the current registrations, and preceding the annual index. Some cross references were listed in the body of the current registrations for an author and in the index for reference from illustrator, translator, joint author, etc. for the entry in the index. For example in the current registration list for 1946, one finds:

> Shute, Nevil, pseud.
> >*see* Norway, Nevil Shute, 1899-

But this reference is not included in the index.

Beginning in 1947, renewals became a separate part, numbered 14A. They were arranged alphabetically with cross references from the name not used to the name under which the copyright information could be found. In 1951, the arrangement again changed so that the *Catalog* for "Books & Pamphlets" contained the following through the January-June 1973 volume:

> Current Registrations
> Renewal Registrations
> Title Index

As more and more copyrights and renewals were granted, the volumes became larger and larger until they were finally published semiannually. From July 1973 through 1977, a system using one index and referring to the copyright or renewal numbers of the main heading in another volume was used. This was and is a cumbersome method for searching.

Chapter 2

In using the *Catalog*, one also must be aware of the author or main entry heading, particularly for prolific writers where there are several pages of entries by title for one author. For example, in the renewal registrations for January-June 1968, there are several pages of renewal entries for *Superman* by Jerome Siegal and Joe Shuster. As a result one may think that there is nothing between Siegal and *Superman*, consequently missing entries for SJ, SK, SL, SM, etc.

There is, however, a cross reference for Joe Shuster to lead the user from the joint author to the main author or heading under which to find the copyright or renewal information.

There are also different ways to alphabetize of which the searcher must be aware. In some legal dictionaries, the word "pro" preceding another word may be arranged before all other words where "pro" is part of the word, or they may all be interfiled. For example, one arrangement may be:

pro bono	[The word "pro" followed by a
pro forma	space precedes all other words
pro hac vice	beginning with the letters "pro,"
probate	(as in *Black's Law Dictionary*,
proceed	rev. 4th ed., 1968.)]
profession	
prohibit	

But another arrangement may be:

probate	["Pro" as a word or prefix
pro bono	letters are interfiled (as in
proceed	*Ballentine's Law Dictionary*,
profession	3d ed., 1969.)]
pro forma	
pro hac vice	
prohibit	

It is the second arrangement above that is used for names beginning with "Du" in the renewal section of the January-June 1968 *Catalog*. An example of some of the names beginning with the letter "D" is:

Dollond, pseud.
Duffus
Du Genestoux
Dull
Dulles
Du Maurier

This interfiled arrangement also applies to a mixture of titles and proper names in the renewals for 1973 through 1977 where, for example, a title beginning with the words "sea gull" follows the name "Seagal." This can create confusion for a searcher who may not realize the difference in the arrangements.

In early library catalog filing rules, *Mc* was filed as *Mac*. But with computerization, *Mc* follows *Maz* as in most phone books. In the 1968 *Catalog*, *Mc* and *Mac* are interfiled as follows:

McCall
MacCampbell
McDermott
MacDonald
Macharg

Therefore, a searcher must be aware of these changes, and examine the alphabetical arrangement carefully, otherwise entries can be missed easily. It is most important to check the opposite way of alphabetizing if the entry is not found in the first manner searched.

Since all materials prior to January 1, 1914 are in the public domain as of December 31, 1988 (1989 minus 75 years), the analysis for the year-by-year renewal search in Part II begins with 1941 (1914 plus 28 minus 1 for the 27th year). The analytical pages for each year in Part II explain the mechanics of using the *Catalog of Copyright Entries* and the changes made in its arrangement through the years. This should aid a searcher to determine, prior to beginning a search, just how the material is organized.

SUMMARY OF PROCEDURE

Rule-of-thumb guidelines:

·Copyright expiration need not be searched if the copyright owner has given permission for publication in any form. Arrangements can be made with the owner for use of the copyrighted material, with or without a fee.

·Ascertain the original copyright date of a work, up to and including December 31, 1977. "(In the case of works originally registered in unpublished form, copyright begins on the date of registration; for published works, copyright begins on the date of first publication.)"[38]

·If there is a question about whether the work has been copyrighted, check the *Catalog* for copyright registration entry. Then begin the search for renewal under the copyright owner listed in the registration entry as described in the example of Burns, Gracie Allen on page 12.

·Check for renewal of copyright in the appropriate part of the *Catalog of Copyright Entries* for the 27th, 28th, and possibly 29th or 30th year from the copyright date.

·Where the copyright owner has changed, which may occur by death or other transfer of registration, cross references will lead the searcher to the correct renewal registration, for example:

>BURNS, GEORGE N.
>   How to become President. See
>   BURNS, GRACIE ALLEN.

•Any copyright obtained prior to January 1, 1978 is subject to renewal or it will expire on December 31 of the 28th year.

•If renewed prior to 1978, and renewal did not expire before September 19, 1962, renewal is extended for 47 years, or a total of 75 years from the original date of copyright.

•If copyright is in its first term on January 1, 1978, copyright must be renewed or it will expire on December 31 of the 28th year.

•If copyright expires, it is lost forever.

•Copyrights as of January 1, 1978 endure for the life of the author plus 50 years. Any work copyrighted in 1978 cannot enter the public domain until possibly 2029, assuming the author died in 1978. In such case copyright would expire on December 31, 2028.[39]

A NOTE OF CAUTION

It should be noted that not all copyright renewal searches are simple. Some are complicated. There are reasons why a copyright renewal might not be published in the *Catalog*. There are occasions when conflicts occur between claimants, and appeals delay the renewal process. It is up to the searcher to determine whether a negative result of a renewal search is in fact a lack of renewal or a delay in listing the renewal in the *Catalog*. An appeal may take years, and one can never be certain about the date of appearance in the *Catalog*. If one is unsure of the results of a search, two alternatives are possible:

1) consult a copyright attorney;
2) search the records in the Copyright Office:
   a) by oneself, as the card catalog and online files in the Copyright Office are open to the public;[40] or
   b) by request to the Copyright Office. For a fee of $10.00 per hour, which covers the search only, not any certificates, photocopies, or other copies of the records, the Copyright Office will perform the search.[41]

Requests can be sent to:

Reference and Bibliography Section, LM-451
Copyright Office
Library of Congress
Washington, DC 20559
(202) 287-6850

When making a request, provide the Copyright Office with information on the author(s), title, year work was published or registered (see above at footnote 38), name of probable copyright owner, and other copyright data.[42]

The Copyright Office is located in the:

Library of Congress
James Madison Memorial Building
101 Independence Avenue, S.E.
Washington, D.C. 20540

PART II

USING THE *CATALOG OF COPYRIGHT ENTRIES*

SAMPLE ENTRY IN THE *CATALOG OF COPYRIGHT ENTRIES*

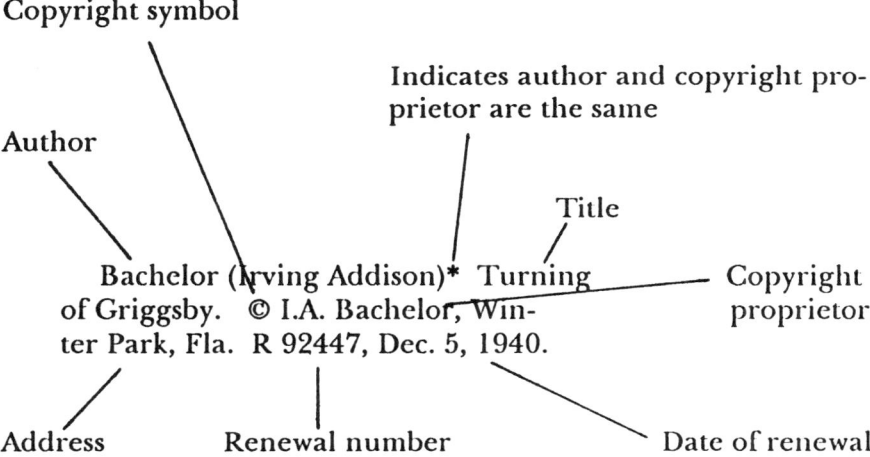

LIST OF ABBREVIATIONS

Copyright Claim Bases:

(A)	author
(C)	child or children of deceased author
(E)	executor(s) of the author
(NK)	next of kin of the author, who is not living
(P)	proprietor of a commercial print or label
(PCB)	proprietor of a work copyrighted by a corporate body other than as assignee or licensee
(PCW)	proprietor of a composite work
(PPW)	proprietor of a posthumous work
(PWH)	proprietor of copyright in a work made for hire
(W)	widow of the author
(WR)	widower of the author

LIST OF ABBREVIATIONS

Other abbreviations:

a.a.d.o.	accepted alternate (or alternative) designation
acc.	accompaniment
adv.	advertisement
a.k.a.	also known as
anon.	anonymous
appl.	application
approx.	approximate, approximately
arr.	arranged, arrangement, arranged by
au.	author
augm.	augmented
b & w	black and white
bull.	bulletin
© (followed by date)	year of publication as given on the copyright notice
©	copyright claimed by
ca.	circa

chap.	chapter, chapters
col.	color, colored
comp.	compiler, compiled by
d.b.a.	doing business as
ed.	edited by, editor, edition
enl.	enlarged
et al.	and others
fold.	folded
ft.	feet
illus.	illustration, illustrations
in.	inches
ips	inches per second
l.	leaf, leaves
min.	minutes
mm.	millimeters
NM	new matter
no.	number
n.p.	no place of publication
1c, 2c	one copy deposited, two copies deposited

Abbreviations

op.	opus
p.	page, pages
prev.	previous
print.	printing
priv. print.	privately printed
pseud.	pseudonym
pty.	propriety
pub.	published
(R)	renewal
reg.	registration
rev.	revised by, revisor, revision
sec.	seconds
ser.	series
si.	silent
s.l.	sine loco (place of publication or printing not known)
suppl.	supplement
t.	tome
t.a.	trading as
ti.	title, titles

tr.   translator

v., vol.   volume, volumes

CATALOG OF COPYRIGHT ENTRIES TO CHECK: BY YEAR

If book was copyrighted in:	You need to check: 27th year	28th year	29th year
1914	1941	1942	1943
1915	1942	1943	1944
1916	1943	1944	1945
1917	1944	1945	1946
1918	1945	1946	1947
1919	1946	1947	1948
1920	1947	1948	1949
1921	1948	1949	1950
1922	1949	1950	1951
1923	1950	1951	1952
1924	1951	1952	1953
1925	1952	1953	1954
1926	1953	1954	1955
1927	1954	1955	1956
1928	1955	1956	1957
1929	1956	1957	1958
1930	1957	1958	1959
1931	1958	1959	1960
1932	1959	1960	1961
1933	1960	1961	1962
1934	1961	1962	1963
1935	1962	1963	1964
1936	1963	1964	1965
1937	1964	1965	1966
1938	1965	1966	1967

If book was copyrighted in:	You need to check: 27th year	28th year	29th year
1939	1966	1967	1968
1940	1967	1968	1969
1941	1968	1969	1970
1942	1969	1970	1971
1943	1970	1971	1972
1944	1971	1972	1973
1945	1972	1973	1974
1946	1973	1974	1975
1947	1974	1975	1976
1948	1975	1976	1977
1949	1976	1977	1978
1950	1977	1978	1979
1951	1978	1979	1980
1952	1979	1980	1981
1953	1980	1981	*
1954	1981	*	*

*not available as of December 1989

YEAR: 1941

NAME: Library of Congress, Copyright Office, *Catalog of Copyright Entries*, Part 1, Group 1, Books Including List of Renewals, 1941, New Series, v. 38, nos. 1-12. (12 pamphlets)

ARRANGEMENT: Arranged alphabetically by author, or if anonymous, by title at the end of each of the twelve monthly pamphlets following the regular copyright entries for that month. Renewals are numbered separately, beginning with number 1, in each monthly pamphlet. An asterisk (*) after the author's name indicates that the author and copyright proprietor are the same. When the author and copyright proprietor are different, the proprietor's name and address are given separately at the end of the title. The "R" number is the renewal number followed by the date of the renewal.

 Sample entry: Bacheller (Irving Addison)* Turning of Griggsby. © I.A. Bacheller, Winter Park, Fla. R 92447, Dec. 5, 1940.
                2

INDEX: Library of Congress, Copyright Office, *Catalog of Copyright Entries*, Part 1, Books, Group 1, New Series, v. 38, Volume Index for the Year 1941. (1 pamphlet)

INDEX ARRANGEMENT: Arranged alphabetically by author, or if anonymous, by title. Renewals are followed by the number of the last copyright entry in the appropriate monthly pamphlet followed by a number in parentheses indicating the number of the renewal entry in the monthly issue. Regular copyright entries are consecutively numbered, eg., 1-750, 751-1498, etc., but renewals are numbered, beginning with number 1, in each monthly pamphlet. For regular copyright entries, the index refers the user to the consecutive number of the entry. In the following sample entry, there are two entries for Bacheller. The (2) following 1398 means a renewal following regular entry number 1398; 8895 is the regular copyright entry for a book by Bacheller.

 Sample entry: Bacheller (I.A.) 1398 (2), 8895.

YEAR: 1942

NAME: Library of Congress, Copyright Office, *Catalog of Copyright Entries*, Part 1, Group 1, Books Including List of Renewals, 1942, New Series, v. 39, nos. 1-12. (12 pamphlets)

ARRANGEMENT: Arranged alphabetically by author, or if anonymous, by title at the end of each of the twelve monthly pamphlets. An asterisk (*) after the author's name indicates that the author and copyright proprietor are the same. When the author and copyright proprietor are different, the proprietor's name and address are given separately at the end of the title. For a sample entry, see 1941.

INDEX: Library of Congress, Copyright Office, *Catalog of Copyright Entries*, Part 1, Books, Group 1, New Series, v. 39, Volume Index for the Year 1942. (1 pamphlet)

INDEX ARRANGEMENT: Arranged alphabetically by author, or if anonymous, by title. Renewals are followed by the number of the last copyright entry in the appropriate monthly pamphlet followed by a number in parentheses indicating the number of the entry in the monthly issue. Regular copyright entries are consecutively numbered, eg., 1-750, 751-1498, etc., but renewals are numbered, beginning with number 1, in each monthly pamphlet. For regular copyright entries, the index refers the user to the consecutive number of the entry. For a sample entry, see 1941.

Part II

YEAR: 1943

NAME: Library of Congress, Copyright Office, *Catalog of Copyright Entries*, Part 1, Group 1, Books Including List of Renewals, 1943, New Series, v. 40, nos. 1-12. (12 pamphlets)

ARRANGEMENT: Arranged alphabetically by author, or if anonymous, by title at the end of each of the twelve monthly pamphlets. An asterisk (*) after the author's name indicates that the author and copyright proprietor are the same. When the author and copyright proprietor are different, the proprietor's name and address are given separately at the end of the title. For a sample entry, see 1941.

INDEX: Library of Congress, Copyright Office, *Catalog of Copyright Entries*, Part 1, Books, Group 1, New Series, v. 40, Volume Index for the Year 1943. (1 pamphlet)

INDEX ARRANGEMENT: Arranged alphabetically by author, or if anonymous, by title. Renewals are followed by the number of the last copyright entry in the appropriate monthly pamphlet followed by a number in parentheses indicating the number of the entry in the monthly issue. Regular copyright entries are consecutively numbered, eg., 1-750, 751-1498, etc., but renewals are numbered, beginning with number 1, in each monthly pamphlet. For regular copyright entries, the index refers the user to the consecutive number of the entry. For a sample entry, see 1941.

YEAR: 1944

NAME: Library of Congress, Copyright Office, *Catalog of Copyright Entries*, Part 1, Group 1, Books Including List of Renewals, 1944, New Series, v. 41, nos. 1-12. (12 pamphlets)

ARRANGEMENT: Arranged alphabetically by author, or if anonymous, by title at the end of each of the twelve monthly pamphlets. An asterisk (*) after the author's name indicates that the author and copyright proprietor are the same. When the author and copyright proprietor are different, the proprietor's name and address are given separately at the end of the title. For a sample entry, see 1941.

INDEX: Library of Congress, Copyright Office, *Catalog of Copyright Entries*, Part 1, Books, Group 1, New Series, v. 41, Volume Index for the Year 1944. (1 pamphlet)

INDEX ARRANGEMENT: Arranged alphabetically by author, or if anonymous, by title. Renewals are followed by the number of the last copyright entry in the appropriate monthly pamphlet followed by a number in parentheses indicating the number of the entry in the monthly issue. Regular copyright entries are consecutively numbered, eg., 1-750, 751-1498, etc., but renewals are numbered, beginning with number 1, in each monthly pamphlet. For regular copyright entries, the index refers the user to the consecutive number of the entry. For a sample entry, see 1941.

Part II

YEAR: 1945

NAME: Library of Congress, Copyright Office, *Catalog of Copyright Entries*, Part 1, Group 1, Books Including List of Renewals, 1945, New Series, v. 42, nos. 1-12. (12 pamphlets)

ARRANGEMENT: Arranged alphabetically by author, or if anonymous, by title at the end of each of the twelve monthly pamphlets. An asterisk (*) after the author's name indicates that the author and copyright proprietor are the same. When the author and copyright proprietor are different, the proprietor's name and address are given separately at the end of the title. For a sample entry, see 1941.

INDEX: Library of Congress, Copyright Office, *Catalog of Copyright Entries*, Part 1, Books, Group 1, New Series, v. 42, Volume Index for the Year 1945. (1 pamphlet)

INDEX ARRANGEMENT: Arranged alphabetically by author, or if anonymous, by title. Renewals are followed by the number of the last copyright entry in the appropriate monthly pamphlet followed by a number in parentheses indicating the number of the entry in the monthly issue. Regular copyright entries are consecutively numbered, eg., 1-750, 751-1498, etc., but renewals are numbered, beginning with number 1, in each monthly pamphlet. For regular copyright entries, the index refers the user to the consecutive number of the entry. For a sample entry, see 1941.

YEAR: 1946

NAME: Library of Congress, Copyright Office, *Catalog of Copyright Entries*, Part 1, Group 1, Books Including List of Renewals and Annual Index, 1946, New Series, v. 43. (1 volume)

ARRANGEMENT: Renewals appear in the second section of this volume. They are arranged alphabetically by the names of the authors of the works renewed, including cross-references from joint authors, etc. Abbreviations, in parentheses, following the name of the renewal owner indicate the basis for the renewal claim as follows: A = author, W = widow of author, WR = widower of author, C = child or children of deceased author, E = executor(s) of author, NK = next of kin of author, PPW = proprietor of a posthumous work, PCW = proprietor of a composite work, PCB = proprietor of a work copyrighted by a corporate body other than as assignee or licensee of the author, PWH = proprietor of copyright in a work made for hire. The date followed by the "A" number is the original date of copyright and the copyright registration number. The "R" number is the renewal number followed by the date of renewal. In the following example, note that the renewal of 30May46 was made during the 28th year of copyright which otherwise would have expired on April 17, 1947. The renewal information was found in the *Catalog of Copyright Entries* for 1946, 27 years from the date of copyright.

Sample entry: Abbott, Austin. Abbott's digest of all
the New York reports, 1918.
© 17Apr19, A525167. R6027, 30May46:
Lawyers co-operative publishing co.
(PCW) Rochester, N. Y.

INDEX: no separate index; self-indexed in Section 2 of the 1946 volume.

INDEX ARRANGEMENT: not applicable.

Part II

YEAR: 1947

NAME: *Catalog of Copyright Entries*, 3rd Series, v. 1, Part 14A, nos. 1-2, Renewal Registrations--Literature, Art, Film, January-December 1947. (1 volume)

ARRANGEMENT: Arranged alphabetically under main heading (author, editor, compiler or title) with brief cross references from joint authors, editors, etc, and titles. Each entry contains the copyright symbol followed by the date of the original copyright, the original registration number, the renewal registration number, date of receipt of renewal application, name of renewal claimant, and a statement of the basis of the renewal claim. For a list of abbreviations of the renewal claim bases, see arrangement section for 1946 or the list of abbreviations on page 25.

Sample entry: ADAMS, GEORGE BURTON. The origin of the English constitution.
Enl. ed. © 15Oct20, A601251;
R25701, 17Nov47; Ruth Adams (C)

INDEX: no separate index.

INDEX ARRANGEMENT: not applicable.

YEAR: 1948

NAME: *Catalog of Copyright Entries*, 3rd Series, v. 2, Part 14A, nos. 1-2, Renewal Registrations--Literature, Art, Film, January-June 1948, July-December 1948. (2 volumes)

ARRANGEMENT: Arranged alphabetically by title with cross references from authors, editors, compilers, etc. Each entry includes the names of authors, illustrators, editors, etc. and the number of volumes and series. The portion of the entry giving the facts of copyright registration begins with the copyright symbol and includes the date of original copyright, original registration number, renewal registration number, date of receipt of renewal application, name of renewal claimant, and basis of renewal claim. For a list of abbreviations for renewal claim bases, see entry for 1946 or the list of abbreviations on page 25.

Sample entry: THE AGE OF INNOCENCE, by Edith Wharton. © 15Oct20, A576993. R26071, 21Nov47, Frederic King (E)

INDEX: no separate index.

INDEX ARRANGEMENT: not applicable.

Part II

YEAR: 1949

NAME: *Catalog of Copyright Entries*, 3rd Series, v. 3, Part 14A, nos. 1-2, Renewal Registrations--Literature, Art, Film, January-June 1949, July-December 1949. (2 volumes)

ARRANGEMENT: Arranged alphabetically by title with cross references from authors, editors, compilers, etc. Each entry includes the names of authors, illustrators, editors, etc. and the number of volumes and series. The portion of the entry giving the facts of copyright registration begins with the copyright symbol and includes the date of original copyright, original registration number, renewal registration number, date of receipt of renewal application, name of renewal claimant, and basis of renewal claim. For a description of abbreviations of renewal claim bases, see entry for 1946 or the list of abbreviations on page 25. For a sample entry, see 1948.

INDEX: no separate index.

INDEX ARRANGEMENT: not applicable.

YEAR: 1950

NAME: *Catalog of Copyright Entries*, 3rd Series, v. 4, Part 14A, nos. 1-2, Renewal Registrations--Literature, Art, Film, January-June 1950, July-December 1950. (2 volumes)

ARRANGEMENT: Arranged alphabetically by title with cross references from authors, editors, compilers, etc. Each entry includes the names of authors, illustrators, editors, etc. and the number of volumes and series. The portion of the entry giving the facts of copyright registration begins with the copyright symbol and includes the date of original copyright, original registration number, renewal registration number, date of receipt of renewal application, name of renewal claimant, and basis of renewal claim. For a description of abbreviations for renewal claim bases, see entry for 1946 or the list of abbreviations on page 25. For a sample entry, see 1948.

INDEX: no separate index.

INDEX ARRANGEMENT: not applicable.

Part II   43

YEAR: 1951

NAME: *Catalog of Copyright Entries*, 3rd Series, v. 5, Part 1A, nos. 1-2, Books, January-June 1951, July-December 1951. (2 volumes)

ARRANGEMENT: *Catalog* contains domestic and foreign books and pamphlets which have been selected for the general collection of the Library of Congress. There are four sections in the *Catalog*: Books, Renewals, Title Index, and Claimant Index. Renewal entries are listed alphabetically by main heading (author, editor, compiler or title) with cross references to joint authors, etc. Renewal entries include the following data: heading, title, names of all authors of renewable matter, edition statement, number of volumes if more than one, and series. The facts of copyright begin with the copyright symbol followed by: a brief statement of the new matter on which copyright is claimed when the information can be secured from the renewal application or the records of the Copyright Office; date of original copyright; original registration number; renewal registration number; date of the receipt of renewal application; name of the renewal claimant; and an abbreviation in parentheses representing the applicant's statement of the basis of his renewal claim.

   Sample entry: ABBOTT, AUSTIN.
                  Digest of all the New York reports,
              1922. © 18May23, A704623. R77831,
              25Apr51, The Lawyers Co-operative
              Pub. Co. (PCW)

INDEX: Includes a title index and a claimant index as part of the main volume. Both are arranged alphabetically.

INDEX ARRANGEMENT: The title index gives the heading under which the complete entry will be found. Each renewal title includes the renewal registration number.

Sample entry: Digest of all the New York
 reports. R77831.
 Abbott, Austin.

The claimant index lists the titles of works of which the claimant is the author or owner. Renewal titles include the renewal registration number.

Sample entry: LAWYERS CO-OPERATIVE
 PUBLISHING COMPANY.
 Abbott, Austin.
 Digest of all the New York
 reports, 1922. R77831.

Part II

YEAR: 1952

NAME: *Catalog of Copyright Entries*, 3rd Series, v. 6, Part 1A, nos. 1-2, Books, January-June 1952, July-December 1952. (2 volumes)

ARRANGEMENT: *Catalog* contains domestic and foreign books and pamphlets which have been selected for the general collection of the Library of Congress. There are four sections in the *Catalog*: Books, Renewals, Title Index, and Claimant Index. Renewal entries are listed alphabetically by main heading (author, editor, compiler or title) with cross references to joint authors, etc. Renewal entries include the following data: heading, title, names of all authors of renewable matter, edition statement, number of volumes if more than one, and series. The facts of copyright begin with the copyright symbol followed by: a brief statement of the new matter on which copyright is claimed when the information can be secured from the renewal application or the records of the Copyright Office; date of original copyright; original registration number; renewal registration number; date of the receipt of renewal application; name of the renewal claimant; and an abbreviation in parentheses representing the applicant's statement of the basis of his renewal claim. For a sample entry, see 1951.

INDEX: Contains an alphabetical title and claimant index in the main volume.

INDEX ARRANGEMENT: The title index gives the heading under which the complete entry will be found. Each renewal title includes the renewal registration number. The claimant index lists the titles of works of which the claimant is the author or owner. Renewal titles include the renewal registration number. For sample entries, see 1951.

DATE: 1953

NAME: *Catalog of Copyright Entries*, 3rd Series, v. 7, Part 1A, nos. 1-2, Books, January-June 1953, July-December 1953. (2 volumes)

ARRANGEMENT: There are three sections in the *Catalog*: Books, Renewals, and Title Index. For renewals, the main entry includes, in addition to the heading, the following: title; names of the authors of renewable matter; edition statement; number of volumes if more than one; and series title. The information relating to the claim of copyright is preceded by the copyright symbol and includes the following: a brief statement of the new matter on which the original copyright was claimed, if available; date of original copyright; original registration number; renewal registration number; date of receipt of the renewal application; and name of the renewal claimant followed by an abbreviation in parentheses representing the claimant's statement of the basis of his renewal claim.

Sample entry: ALABAMA. SUPREME COURT.
  Report of cases argued and determined
   in the Supreme Court of Alabama.
   Vol. 213, October terms, 1924-1925,
   1925-1926. By Noble H. Seay,
   reporter. © 17Feb26, A891337.
   R109788, 3Apr53, State of Alabama (PWH)

INDEX: An alphabetical title index is included in the main volume.

INDEX ARRANGEMENT: Below each title, the heading under which the complete entry will be found is given. Renewal titles are distinguished by the symbol (R).

Sample entry: Report of cases argued and de-
    termined in the Supreme
    Court of Alabama. (R)
   Alabama. Supreme Court.

Part II 47

YEAR: 1954

NAME: *Catalog of Copyright Entries*, 3rd Series, v. 8, Part 1, nos. 1-2, Books and Pamphlets Including Serials and Contributions to Periodicals, January-June 1954, July-December 1954. (2 volumes)

ARRANGEMENT: There are three sections in the *Catalog*: Books, Renewals, and Title Index. For renewals, the main entry includes, in addition to the heading, the following: title; names of the authors of renewable matter; edition statement; number of volumes if more than one; and series title. The information relating to the claim of copyright is preceded by the copyright symbol and includes the following: a brief statement of the new matter on which the original copyright was claimed, if available; date of original copyright; original registration number; renewal registration number; date of receipt of the renewal application; and name of the renewal claimant followed by an abbreviation in parentheses representing the claimant's statement of the basis of his renewal claim. For a sample entry, see 1953.

INDEX: An alphabetical title index is included in the main volume.

INDEX ARRANGEMENT: Below each title, the heading under which the complete entry will be found is given. Renewal titles are distinguished by the symbol (R). For a sample entry, see 1953.

YEAR: 1955

NAME: *Catalog of Copyright Entries*, 3rd Series, v. 9, Part 1, nos. 1-2, Books and Pamphlets Including Serials and Contributions to Periodicals, January-June 1955, July-December 1955. (2 volumes)

ARRANGEMENT: There are three sections in the *Catalog*: Books, Renewals, and Title Index. For renewals, the main entry includes, in addition to the heading, the following: title; names of the authors of renewable matter; edition statement; number of volumes if more than one; and series title. The information relating to the claim of copyright is preceded by the copyright symbol and includes the following: a brief statement of the new matter on which the original copyright was claimed, if available; date of original copyright; original registration number; renewal registration number; date of receipt of the renewal application; and name of the renewal claimant followed by an abbreviation in parentheses representing the claimant's statement of the basis of his renewal claim. For a sample entry, see 1953.

INDEX: An alphabetical title index is included in the main volume.

INDEX ARRANGEMENT: Below each title, the heading under which the complete entry will be found is given. Renewal titles are distinguished by the symbol (R). For a sample entry, see 1953.

Part II

YEAR: 1956

NAME: *Catalog of Copyright Entries*, 3rd Series, v. 10, Part 1, nos. 1-2, Books and Pamphlets Including Serials and Contributions to Periodicals, January-June 1956, July-December 1956. (2 volumes)

ARRANGEMENT: There are three sections in the *Catalog*: Books, Renewals, and Title Index. For renewals, the main entry includes, in addition to the heading, the following: title; names of the authors of renewable matter; edition statement; number of volumes if more than one; and series title. The information relating to the claim of copyright is preceded by the copyright symbol and includes the following: a brief statement of the new matter on which the original copyright was claimed, if available; date of original copyright; original registration number; renewal registration number; date of receipt of the renewal application; and name of the renewal claimant followed by an abbreviation in parentheses representing the claimant's statement of the basis of his renewal claim. For a sample entry, see 1953.

INDEX: An alphabetical title index is included in the main volume.

INDEX ARRANGEMENT: Below each title, the heading under which the complete entry will be found is given. Renewal titles are distinguished by the symbol (R). For a sample entry, see 1953.

YEAR: 1957

NAME: *Catalog of Copyright Entries*, 3rd Series, v. 11, Part 1, nos. 1-2, Books and Pamphlets Including Serials and Contributions to Periodicals, January-June 1957, July-December 1957. (2 volumes)

ARRANGEMENT: There are three sections in the *Catalog*: Books, Renewals, and Title Index. For renewals, the main entry includes, in addition to the heading, the following: title; names of the authors of renewable matter; edition statement; number of volumes if more than one; and series title. The information relating to the claim of copyright is preceded by the copyright symbol and includes the following: a brief statement of the new matter on which the original copyright was claimed, if available; date of original copyright; original registration number; renewal registration number; date of receipt of the renewal application; and name of the renewal claimant followed by an abbreviation in parentheses representing the claimant's statement of the basis of his renewal claim. For a sample entry, see 1953.

INDEX: An alphabetical title index is included in the main volume.

INDEX ARRANGEMENT: Below each title, the heading under which the complete entry will be found is given. Renewal titles are distinguished by the symbol (R). For a sample entry, see 1953.

YEAR: 1958

NAME: *Catalog of Copyright Entries*, 3rd Series, v. 12, Part 1, nos. 1-2, Books and Pamphlets Including Serials and Contributions to Periodicals, January-June 1958, July-December 1958. (2 volumes)

ARRANGEMENT: There are three sections in the *Catalog*: Books, Renewals, and Title Index. For renewals, the main entry includes, in addition to the heading, the following: title; names of the authors of renewable matter; edition statement; number of volumes if more than one; and series title. The information relating to the claim of copyright is preceded by the copyright symbol and includes the following: a brief statement of the new matter on which the original copyright was claimed, if available; date of original copyright; original registration number; renewal registration number; date of receipt of the renewal application; and name of the renewal claimant followed by an abbreviation in parentheses representing the claimant's statement of the basis of his renewal claim. For a sample entry, see 1953.

INDEX: An alphabetical title index is included in the main volume.

INDEX ARRANGEMENT: Below each title, the heading under which the complete entry will be found is given. Renewal titles are distinguished by the symbol (R). For a sample entry, see 1953.

YEAR: 1959

NAME: *Catalog of Copyright Entries*, 3rd Series, v. 13, Part 1, nos. 1-2, Books and Pamphlets Including Serials and Contributions to Periodicals, January-June 1959, July-December 1959. (2 volumes)

ARRANGEMENT: There are three sections in the *Catalog*: Books, Renewals, and Title Index. For renewals, the main entry includes, in addition to the heading, the following: title; names of the authors of renewable matter; edition statement; number of volumes if more than one; and series title. The information relating to the claim of copyright is preceded by the copyright symbol and includes the following: a brief statement of the new matter on which the original copyright was claimed, if available; date of original copyright; original registration number; renewal registration number; date of receipt of the renewal application; and name of the renewal claimant followed by an abbreviation in parentheses representing the claimant's statement of the basis of his renewal claim. For a sample entry, see 1953.

INDEX: An alphabetical title index is included in the main volume.

INDEX ARRANGEMENT: Below each title, the heading under which the complete entry will be found is given. Renewal titles are distinguished by the symbol (R). For a sample entry, see 1953.

Part II 53

YEAR: 1960

NAME: *Catalog of Copyright Entries*, 3rd Series, v. 14, Part 1, nos. 1-2, Books and Pamphlets Including Serials and Contributions to Periodicals, January-June 1960, July-December 1960. (2 volumes)

ARRANGEMENT: There are three sections in the *Catalog*: Books, Renewals, and Title Index. For renewals, the main entry includes, in addition to the heading, the following: title; names of the authors of renewable matter; edition statement; number of volumes if more than one; and series title. The information relating to the claim of copyright is preceded by the copyright symbol and includes the following: a brief statement of the new matter on which the original copyright was claimed, if available; date of original copyright; original registration number; renewal registration number; date of receipt of the renewal application; and name of the renewal claimant followed by an abbreviation in parentheses representing the claimant's statement of the basis of his renewal claim. For a sample entry, see 1953.

INDEX: An alphabetical title index is included in the main volume.

INDEX ARRANGEMENT: Below each title, the heading under which the complete entry will be found is given. Renewal titles are distinguished by the symbol (R). For a sample entry, see 1953.

YEAR: 1961

NAME: *Catalog of Copyright Entries*, 3rd Series, v. 15, Part 1, nos. 1-2, Books and Pamphlets Including Serials and Contributions to Periodicals, January-June 1961, July-December 1961. (2 volumes)

ARRANGEMENT: There are three sections in the *Catalog*: Books, Renewals, and Title Index. For renewals, the main entry includes, in addition to the heading, the following: title; names of the authors of renewable matter; edition statement; number of volumes if more than one; and series title. The information relating to the claim of copyright is preceded by the copyright symbol and includes the following: a brief statement of the new matter on which the original copyright was claimed, if available; date of original copyright; original registration number; renewal registration number; date of receipt of the renewal application; and name of the renewal claimant followed by an abbreviation in parentheses representing the claimant's statement of the basis of his renewal claim. For a sample entry, see 1953.

INDEX: An alphabetical title index is included in the main volume.

INDEX ARRANGEMENT: Below each title, the heading under which the complete entry will be found is given. Renewal titles are distinguished by the symbol (R). For a sample entry, see 1953.

YEAR: 1962

NAME: *Catalog of Copyright Entries*, 3rd Series, v. 16, Part 1, nos. 1-2, Books and Pamphlets Including Serials and Contributions to Periodicals, January-June 1962, July-December 1962. (2 volumes)

ARRANGEMENT: There are three sections in the *Catalog*: Books, Renewals, and Title Index. For renewals, the main entry includes, in addition to the heading, the following: title; names of the authors of renewable matter; edition statement; number of volumes if more than one; and series title. The information relating to the claim of copyright is preceded by the copyright symbol and includes the following: a brief statement of the new matter on which the original copyright was claimed, if available; date of original copyright; original registration number; renewal registration number; date of receipt of the renewal application; and name of the renewal claimant followed by an abbreviation in parentheses representing the claimant's statement of the basis of his renewal claim. For a sample entry, see 1953.

INDEX: An alphabetical title index is included in the main volume.

INDEX ARRANGEMENT: Below each title, the heading under which the complete entry will be found is given. Renewal titles are distinguished by the symbol (R). For a sample entry, see 1953.

YEAR: 1963

NAME: *Catalog of Copyright Entries*, 3rd Series, v. 17, Part 1, nos. 1-2, Books and Pamphlets Including Serials and Contributions to Periodicals, January-June 1963, July-December 1963. (2 volumes)

ARRANGEMENT: There are three sections in the *Catalog*: Books, Renewals, and Title Index. For renewals, the main entry includes, in addition to the heading, the following: title; names of the authors of renewable matter; edition statement; number of volumes if more than one; and series title. The information relating to the claim of copyright is preceded by the copyright symbol and includes the following: a brief statement of the new matter on which the original copyright was claimed, if available; date of original copyright; original registration number; renewal registration number; date of receipt of the renewal application; and name of the renewal claimant followed by an abbreviation in parentheses representing the claimant's statement of the basis of his renewal claim. For a sample entry, see 1953.

INDEX: An alphabetical title index is included in the main volume.

INDEX ARRANGEMENT: Below each title, the heading under which the complete entry will be found is given. Renewal titles are distinguished by the symbol (R). For a sample entry, see 1953.

YEAR: 1964

NAME: *Catalog of Copyright Entries*, 3rd Series, v. 18, Part 1, nos. 1-2, Books and Pamphlets Including Serials and Contributions to Periodicals, January-June 1964, July-December 1964. (2 volumes)

ARRANGEMENT: There are three sections in the *Catalog*: Books, Renewals, and Title Index. For renewals, the main entry includes, in addition to the heading, the following: title; names of the authors of renewable matter; edition statement; number of volumes if more than one; and series title. The information relating to the claim of copyright is preceded by the copyright symbol and includes the following: a brief statement of the new matter on which the original copyright was claimed, if available; date of original copyright; original registration number; renewal registration number; date of receipt of the renewal application; and name of the renewal claimant followed by an abbreviation in parentheses representing the claimant's statement of the basis of his renewal claim. For a sample entry, see 1953.

INDEX: An alphabetical title index is included in the main volume.

INDEX ARRANGEMENT: Below each title, the heading under which the complete entry will be found is given. Renewal titles are distinguished by the symbol (R). For a sample entry, see 1953.

YEAR: 1965

NAME: *Catalog of Copyright Entries*, 3rd Series, v. 19, Part 1, nos. 1-2, Books and Pamphlets Including Serials and Contributions to Periodicals, January-June 1965, July-December 1965. (2 volumes)

ARRANGEMENT: There are three sections in the *Catalog*: Books, Renewals, and Title Index. For renewals, the main entry includes, in addition to the heading, the following: title; names of the authors of renewable matter; edition statement; number of volumes if more than one; and series title. The information relating to the claim of copyright is preceded by the copyright symbol and includes the following: a brief statement of the new matter on which the original copyright was claimed, if available; date of original copyright; original registration number; renewal registration number; date of receipt of the renewal application; and name of the renewal claimant followed by an abbreviation in parentheses representing the claimant's statement of the basis of his renewal claim. For a sample entry, see 1953.

INDEX: An alphabetical title index is included in the main volume.

INDEX ARRANGEMENT: Below each title, the heading under which the complete entry will be found is given. Renewal titles are distinguished by the symbol (R). For a sample entry, see 1953.

Part II

YEAR: 1966

NAME: *Catalog of Copyright Entries*, 3rd Series, v. 20, Part 1, nos. 1-2, Section 1, Books and Pamphlets Including Serials and Contributions to Periodicals, Current and Renewal Registrations, January-June 1966, July-December 1966. (2 volumes)

ARRANGEMENT: Beginning in 1966, the title index is separate from the *Catalog* of current and renewal registrations. There are three sections in the *Catalog*: Books, Renewals, and Title Index. For renewals, the main entry includes, in addition to the heading, the following: title; names of the authors of renewable matter; edition statement; number of volumes if more than one; and series title. The information relating to the claim of copyright is preceded by the copyright symbol and includes the following: a brief statement of the new matter on which the original copyright was claimed, if available; date of original copyright; original registration number; renewal registration number; date of receipt of the renewal application; and name of the renewal claimant followed by an abbreviation in parentheses representing the claimant's statement of the basis of his renewal claim. For a sample entry, see 1953.

INDEX: *Catalog of Copyright Entries*, 3rd Series, v. 20, Part 1, nos. 1-2, Section 2, Books and Pamphlets Including Serials and Contributions to Periodicals, Title Index, January-June 1966, July-December 1966. (2 volumes)

INDEX ARRANGEMENT: Below each title, the heading under which the complete entry will be found is given. Renewal titles are distinguished by the symbol (R). For a sample entry, see 1953.

YEAR: 1967

NAME: *Catalog of Copyright Entries*, 3rd Series, v. 21, Part 1, nos. 1-2, Section 1, Books and Pamphlets Including Serials and Contributions to Periodicals, Current and Renewal Registrations, January-June 1967, July-December 1967. (2 volumes)

ARRANGEMENT: Beginning in 1966, the title index is separate from the *Catalog* of current and renewal registrations. There are three sections in the *Catalog*: Books, Renewals, and Title Index. For renewals, the main entry includes, in addition to the heading, the following: title; names of the authors of renewable matter; edition statement; number of volumes if more than one; and series title. The information relating to the claim of copyright is preceded by the copyright symbol and includes the following: a brief statement of the new matter on which the original copyright was claimed, if available; date of original copyright; original registration number; renewal registration number; date of receipt of the renewal application; and name of the renewal claimant followed by an abbreviation in parentheses representing the claimant's statement of the basis of his renewal claim. For a sample entry, see 1953.

INDEX: *Catalog of Copyright Entries*, 3rd Series, v. 21, Part 1, nos. 1-2, Section 2, Books and Pamphlets Including Serials and Contributions to Periodicals, Title Index, January-June 1967, July-December 1967. (2 volumes)

INDEX ARRANGEMENT: Below each title, the heading under which the complete entry will be found is given. Renewal titles are distinguished by the symbol (R). For a sample entry, see 1953.

YEAR: 1968

NAME: *Catalog of Copyright Entries*, 3rd Series, v. 22, Part 1, nos. 1-2, Section 1, Books and Pamphlets Including Serials and Contributions to Periodicals, Current and Renewal Registrations, January-June 1968, July-December 1968. (2 volumes)

ARRANGEMENT: Beginning in 1966, the title index is separate from the *Catalog* of current and renewal registrations. There are three sections in the *Catalog*: Books, Renewals, and Title Index. For renewals, the main entry includes, in addition to the heading, the following: title; names of the authors of renewable matter; edition statement; number of volumes if more than one; and series title. The information relating to the claim of copyright is preceded by the copyright symbol and includes the following: a brief statement of the new matter on which the original copyright was claimed, if available; date of original copyright; original registration number; renewal registration number; date of receipt of the renewal application; and name of the renewal claimant followed by an abbreviation in parentheses representing the claimant's statement of the basis of his renewal claim. For a sample entry, see 1953.

INDEX: *Catalog of Copyright Entries*, 3rd Series, v. 22, Part 1, nos. 1-2, Section 2, Books and Pamphlets Including Serials and Contributions to Periodicals, Title Index, January-June 1968, July-December 1968. (2 volumes)

INDEX ARRANGEMENT: Below each title, the heading under which the complete entry will be found is given. Renewal titles are distinguished by the symbol (R). For a sample entry, see 1953.

YEAR: 1969

NAME: *Catalog of Copyright Entries*, 3rd Series, v. 23, Part 1, nos. 1-2, Section 1, Books and Pamphlets Including Serials and Contributions to Periodicals, Current and Renewal Registrations, January-June 1969, July-December 1969. (2 volumes)

ARRANGEMENT: Beginning in 1966, the title index is separate from the *Catalog* of current and renewal registrations. There are three sections in the *Catalog*: Books, Renewals, and Title Index. For renewals, the main entry includes, in addition to the heading, the following: title; names of the authors of renewable matter; edition statement; number of volumes if more than one; and series title. The information relating to the claim of copyright is preceded by the copyright symbol and includes the following: a brief statement of the new matter on which the original copyright was claimed, if available; date of original copyright; original registration number; renewal registration number; date of receipt of the renewal application; and name of the renewal claimant followed by an abbreviation in parentheses representing the claimant's statement of the basis of his renewal claim. For a sample entry, see 1953.

INDEX: *Catalog of Copyright Entries*, 3rd Series, v. 23, Part 1, nos. 1-2, Section 2, Books and Pamphlets Including Serials and Contributions to Periodicals, Title Index, January-June 1969, July-December 1969. (2 volumes)

INDEX ARRANGEMENT: Below each title, the heading under which the complete entry will be found is given. Renewal titles are distinguished by the symbol (R). For a sample entry, see 1953.

YEAR: 1970

NAME: *Catalog of Copyright Entries*, 3rd Series, v. 24, Part 1, nos. 1-2, Section 1, Books and Pamphlets Including Serials and Contributions to Periodicals, Current and Renewal Registrations, January-June 1970, July-December 1970. (2 volumes)

ARRANGEMENT: Beginning in 1966, the title index is separate from the *Catalog* of current and renewal registrations. There are three sections in the *Catalog*: Books, Renewals, and Title Index. For renewals, the main entry includes, in addition to the heading, the following: title; names of the authors of renewable matter; edition statement; number of volumes if more than one; and series title. The information relating to the claim of copyright is preceded by the copyright symbol and includes the following: a brief statement of the new matter on which the original copyright was claimed, if available; date of original copyright; original registration number; renewal registration number; date of receipt of the renewal application; and name of the renewal claimant followed by an abbreviation in parentheses representing the claimant's statement of the basis of his renewal claim. For a sample entry, see 1953.

INDEX: *Catalog of Copyright Entries*, 3rd Series, v. 24, Part 1, nos. 1-2, Section 2, Books and Pamphlets Including Serials and Contributions to Periodicals, Title Index, January-June 1970, July-December 1970. (2 volumes)

INDEX ARRANGEMENT: Below each title, the heading under which the complete entry will be found is given. Renewal titles are distinguished by the symbol (R). For a sample entry, see 1953.

YEAR: 1971

NAME: *Catalog of Copyright Entries*, 3rd Series, v. 25, Part 1, nos. 1-2, Section 1, Books and Pamphlets Including Serials and Contributions to Periodicals, Current and Renewal Registrations, January-June 1971, July-December 1971. (2 volumes)

ARRANGEMENT: Beginning in 1966, the title index is separate from the *Catalog* of current and renewal registrations. There are three sections in the *Catalog*: Books, Renewals, and Title Index. For renewals, the main entry includes, in addition to the heading, the following: title; names of the authors of renewable matter; edition statement; number of volumes if more than one; and series title. The information relating to the claim of copyright is preceded by the copyright symbol and includes the following: a brief statement of the new matter on which the original copyright was claimed, if available; date of original copyright; original registration number; renewal registration number; date of receipt of the renewal application; and name of the renewal claimant followed by an abbreviation in parentheses representing the claimant's statement of the basis of his renewal claim. For a sample entry, see 1953.

INDEX: *Catalog of Copyright Entries*, 3rd Series, v. 25, Part 1, nos. 1-2, Section 2, Books and Pamphlets Including Serials and Contributions to Periodicals, Title Index, January-June 1971, July-December 1971. (2 volumes)

INDEX ARRANGEMENT: Below each title, the heading under which the complete entry will be found is given. Renewal titles are distinguished by the symbol (R). For a sample entry, see 1953.

Part II 65

YEAR: 1972

NAME: *Catalog of Copyright Entries*, 3rd Series, v. 26, Part 1, nos. 1-2, Section 2, Books and Pamphlets Including Serials and Contributions to Periodicals, Current Registrations M-Z, Renewal Registrations, January-June 1972, July-December 1972. (2 volumes)

ARRANGEMENT: Beginning in 1966, the title index is separate from the *Catalog* of current and renewal registrations. There are three sections in the *Catalog*: Books, Renewals, and Title Index. For renewals, the main entry includes, in addition to the heading, the following: title; names of the authors of renewable matter; edition statement; number of volumes if more than one; and series title. The information relating to the claim of copyright is preceded by the copyright symbol and includes the following: a brief statement of the new matter on which the original copyright was claimed, if available; date of original copyright; original registration number; renewal registration number; date of receipt of the renewal application; and name of the renewal claimant followed by an abbreviation in parentheses representing the claimant's statement of the basis of his renewal claim. For a sample entry, see 1953.

INDEX: *Catalog of Copyright Entries*, 3rd Series, v. 26, Part 1, nos. 1-2, Section 3, Books and Pamphlets Including Serials and Contributions to Periodicals, Title Index, January-June 1972, July-December 1972. (2 volumes)

INDEX ARRANGEMENT: Below each title, the heading under which the complete entry will be found is given. Renewal titles are distinguished by the symbol (R). For a sample entry, see 1953.

YEAR: January-June 1973

NAME: *Catalog of Copyright Entries*, 3rd Series, v. 27, Part 1, no. 1, Section 2, Books and Pamphlets Including Serials and Contributions to Periodicals, Current Registrations M-Z, Renewal Registrations, January-June 1973. (1 volume)

ARRANGEMENT: Beginning in 1966, the title index is separate from the *Catalog* of current and renewal registrations. There are three sections in the *Catalog*: Books, Renewals, and Title Index. For renewals, the main entry includes, in addition to the heading, the following: title; names of the authors of renewable matter; edition statement; number of volumes if more than one; and series title. The information relating to the claim of copyright is preceded by the copyright symbol and includes the following: a brief statement of the new matter on which the original copyright was claimed, if available; date of original copyright; original registration number; renewal registration number; date of receipt of the renewal application; and name of the renewal claimant followed by an abbreviation in parentheses representing the claimant's statement of the basis of his renewal claim. For a sample entry, see 1953.

INDEX: *Catalog of Copyright Entries*, v. 27, Part 1, no. 1, Section 3, Books and Pamphlets Including Serials and Contributions to Periodicals, Title Index, January-June 1973. (1 volume)

INDEX ARRANGEMENT: Below each title, the heading under which the complete entry will be found is given. Renewal titles are distinguished by the symbol (R). For a sample entry, see 1953.

Part II

YEAR: July-December 1973

NAME: *Catalog of Copyright Entries*, 3rd Series, v. 27, Part 1, no. 2, Section 1, Books and Pamphlets Including Serials and Contributions to Periodicals, Current and Renewal Registrations, July-December 1973. (1 volume)

ARRANGEMENT: Renewals are arranged by registration number. As renewal registrations are numbered continuously for all classes, there will be breaks in the sequence for any given type of material. The original date of publication and registration number precede the name of the claimant of the renewal registration which is followed by a statement in parentheses, usually abbreviated, giving the basis of the renewal claim. For a list of abbreviations for renewal claim bases, see the list of abbreviations on page 25.

Sample entry: R554972.
   National interest and international
   cartels. By Charles R. Whittlesey.
   © 4Jun46; A3272. Charles R. Whittlesey (A); 2Jul73; R554972.

INDEX: *Catalog of Copyright Entries*, 3rd Series, v. 27, Part 1, no. 2, Section 2, Books and Pamphlets Including Serials and Contributions to Periodicals, Index, July-December 1973. (1 volume)

INDEX ARRANGEMENT: The index is arranged by title and name of current and renewal entries. Below each index item is the registration number under which the main entry may be found.

Sample entry: National interest and international
   cartels.
   R554972.

YEAR: 1974

NAME: *Catalog of Copyright Entries*, 3rd Series, v. 28, Part 1, nos. 1-2, Section 2, Books and Pamphlets Including Contributions to Periodicals, Current and Renewal Registrations, January-June 1974, July-December 1974. (2 volumes)

ARRANGEMENT: Renewals are arranged by registration number. As renewal registrations are numbered continuously for all classes, there will be breaks in the sequence for any given type of material. The original date of publication and registration number precede the name of the claimant of the renewal registration which is followed by a statement in parentheses, usually abbreviated, giving the basis of the renewal claim. For a sample entry, see July-December 1973.

INDEX: *Catalog of Copyright Entries*, 3rd Series, v. 28, Part 1, nos. 1-2, Section 1, Books and Pamphlets Including Contributions to Periodicals, Index, January-June 1974, July-December 1974. (2 volumes)

INDEX ARRANGEMENT: The index is arranged by title and name of current and renewal entries. Below each index item is the registration number under which the main entry may be found. For a sample entry, see July-December 1973.

YEAR: 1975

NAME: *Catalog of Copyright Entries*, 3rd Series, v. 29, Part 1, nos. 1-2, Section 2, Books and Pamphlets Including Contributions to Periodicals, Current and Renewal Registrations, January-June 1975, July-December 1975. (2 volumes)

ARRANGEMENT: Renewals are arranged by registration number. As renewal registrations are numbered continuously for all classes, there will be breaks in the sequence for any given type of material. The original date of publication and registration number precede the name of the claimant of the renewal registration, which is followed by a statement in parentheses, usually abbreviated, giving the basis of the renewal claim. For a sample entry, see July-December 1973.

INDEX: *Catalog of Copyright Entries*, 3rd Series, v. 29, Part 1, nos. 1-2, Section 1, Books and Pamphlets Including Serials and Contributions to Periodicals, Index, January-June 1975, July-December 1975. (2 volumes)

INDEX ARRANGEMENT: The index is arranged by title and name of current and renewal entries. Below each index item is the registration number under which the main entry may be found. Beginning in 1975, references to pages in the Current and Renewal Registration section, Section 2, are given.

    Sample entry: Aaron, Muriel.
                  R599126............3120

YEAR: 1976

NAME: *Catalog of Copyright Entries*, 3rd Series, v. 30, Part 1, nos. 1-2, Section 2, Books and Pamphlets Including Serials and Contributions to Periodicals, Current and Renewal Registrations, January-June, 1976 July-December 1976. (2 volumes)

ARRANGEMENT: Renewals are arranged by registration number. As renewal registrations are numbered continuously for all classes, there will be breaks in the sequence for any given type of material. The original date of publication and registration number precede the name of the claimant of the renewal registration, which is followed by a statement in parentheses, usually abbreviated, giving the basis of the renewal claim. For a sample entry, see July-December 1973.

INDEX: *Catalog of Copyright Entries*, 3rd Series, v. 30, Part 1, nos. 1-2, Section 1, Books and Pamphlets Including Serials and Contributions to Periodicals, Index, January-June 1976, July-December 1976. (2 volumes)

INDEX ARRANGEMENT: The index is arranged by title and name of current and renewal entries. Below each index term is the registration number under which the main entry may be found. Beginning in 1975, references to pages in the Current and Renewal Registration section, Section 2, are given. For a sample entry, see 1975.

Part II

YEAR: 1977

NAME: *Catalog of Copyright Entries*, 3rd Series, v. 31, Part 1, nos. 1-2, Section 2, Books and Pamphlets Including Serials and Contributions to Periodicals, Current and Renewal Registrations, January-June 1977, July-December 1977. (2 volumes)

ARRANGEMENT: Renewals are arranged by registration number. As renewal registrations are numbered continuously for all classes, there will be breaks in the sequence for any given type of material. The original date of publication and registration number precede the name of the claimant of the renewal registration, which is followed by a statement in parentheses, usually abbreviated, giving the basis of the renewal claim. For a sample entry, see July-December 1973.

INDEX: *Catalog of Copyright Entries*, 3rd Series, v. 31, Part 1, nos. 1-2, Section 1, Books and Pamphlets Including Serials and Contributions to Periodicals, Index, January-June 1977, July-December 1977. (2 volumes)

INDEX ARRANGEMENT: The index is arranged by title and name of current and renewal entries. Below each index term is the registration number under which the main entry may be found. Beginning in 1975, references to pages in the Current and Renewal Registration section, Section 2, are given. For a sample entry, see 1975.

YEAR: 1978

NAME: *Catalog of Copyright Entries*, 4th Series, v. 1, Part 8, nos. 1-2, Renewals, January-June 1978, July-December 1978. (2 volumes)

ARRANGEMENT: Part 8 lists all renewal registrations made during the period covered by the issue. Each entry includes: title, followed by subtitle and/or descriptive statements; names of authors, including editors, translators, etc.; edition statement; series statement; additional titles included in the renewal application; notes; statement that the work was published as a contribution to a periodical, serial, or other composite work; brief statement of the new matter on which the copyright was claimed, preceded by the abbreviation NM, if available in the renewal application; copyright symbol; date of original copyright; original registration number; name of the renewal claimant followed by a statement in parentheses giving the basis for the renewal claim; effective date of renewal registration; and renewal registration number.

 Sample entry: ADVANCE CALIFORNIA REPORTS.
   Advance California reports. Vol. 11,
  no. 23. © 6Jun50; AA155224.
  Bancroft-Whitney Company (PWH); 24Mar78;
  RE 1-583.

INDEX: The main volume contains a name index.

INDEX ARRANGEMENT: The name index is alphabetical by renewal claimant, author, and other names associated with the renewal registration.

 Sample entry: Bancroft-Whitney Company.
   Advance California reports.
  (RE 1-583.)

Part II

YEAR: 1979

NAME: *Catalog of Copyright Entries*, 4th Series, v. 2, Part 8, nos. 1-2, Renewals, January-June 1979, July-December 1979. (microfiche)

ARRANGEMENT: Beginning with 1979, the paper catalogs were replaced by microfiche of extremely poor quality. The quality is so poor that it is often difficult to determine what is included on the microfiche. Entries are arranged alphabetically and include the following information: title, followed by subtitle and/or descriptive statements; names of authors, including editors, translators, etc.; edition statement; series statement; additional titles included in the renewal application; notes; statement that the work was published as a contribution to a periodical, serial, or other composite work; brief statement of the new matter on which the copyright was claimed, preceded by the abbreviation NM, if available in the renewal application; copyright symbol; date of original copyright; original registration number; name of the renewal claimant followed by a statement in parentheses giving the basis for the renewal claim; effective date of renewal registration; and renewal registration number. For a sample entry, see 1978.

INDEX: Beginning with 1979, there is no separate index to the *Catalog of Copyright Entries*.

INDEX ARRANGEMENT: Each microfiche contains an alphabetical list, by main entry, of items on that fiche. Each frame of the fiche is numbered, eg., B1, B2, etc. - B18, C1, C2, etc. - C18, and the alphabetical list indicates which frame one must look at to check copyright renewal. Entries are grouped by frame, eg., all frame 1s are together, eg., B1, C1, etc. - P1.

Sample entry: D3 THUS DO YOU BETRAY
E3 TIL I WALTZ AGAIN

YEAR: 1980

NAME: *Catalog of Copyright Entries*, 4th Series, v. 3, Part 8, nos. 1-2, Renewals, January-June 1980, July-December 1980. (microfiche)

ARRANGEMENT: Beginning with 1979, the paper catalogs were replaced by microfiche of extremely poor quality. The quality is so poor that it is often difficult to determine what is included on the microfiche. Entries are arranged alphabetically and include the following information: title, followed by subtitle and/or descriptive statements; names of authors, including editors, translators, etc.; edition statement; series statement; additional titles included in the renewal application; notes; statement that the work was published as a contribution to a periodical, serial, or other composite work; brief statement of the new matter on which the copyright was claimed, preceded by the abbreviation NM, if available in the renewal application; copyright symbol; date of original copyright; original registration number; name of the renewal claimant followed by a statement in parentheses giving the basis for the renewal claim; effective date of renewal registration; and renewal registration number. For a sample entry, see 1978.

INDEX: Beginning with 1979, there is no separate index to the *Catalog of Copyright Entries*.

INDEX ARRANGEMENT: Each microfiche contains an alphabetical list, by main entry, of items on that fiche. Each frame of the fiche is numbered, eg., B1, B2, etc. - B18, C1, C2, etc. - C18, and the alphabetical list indicates which frame one must look at to check copyright renewal. Entries are grouped by frame, eg., all frame 1s are together, eg., B1, C1, etc. - P1. For a sample entry, see 1979.

YEAR: 1981

NAME: *Catalog of Copyright Entries*, 4th Series, v. 4, Part 8, no. 1-2, Renewals, January-June 1981, July-December 1981. (microfiche)

ARRANGEMENT: Beginning with 1979, the paper catalogs were replaced by microfiche of extremely poor quality. The quality is so poor that it is often difficult to determine what is included on the microfiche. Entries are arranged alphabetically and include the following information: title, followed by subtitle and/or descriptive statements; names of authors, including editors, translators, etc.; edition statement; series statement; additional titles included in the renewal application; notes; statement that the work was published as a contribution to a periodical, serial, or other composite work; brief statement of the new matter on which the copyright was claimed, preceded by the abbreviation NM, if available in the renewal application; copyright symbol; date of original copyright; original registration number; name of the renewal claimant followed by a statement in parentheses giving the basis for the renewal claim; effective date of renewal registration; and renewal registration number. For a sample entry, see 1978.

INDEX: Beginning with 1979, there is no separate index to the *Catalog of Copyright Entries*.

INDEX ARRANGEMENT: Each microfiche contains an alphabetical list, by main entry, of items on that fiche. Each frame of the fiche is numbered, eg., B1, B2, etc. - B18, C1, C2, etc. - C18, and the alphabetical list indicates which frame one must look at to check copyright renewal. Entries are grouped by frame, eg., all frame 1s are together, eg., B1, C1, etc. - P1. For a sample entry, see 1979.

FOOTNOTES

[1]U.S. Copyright Office. Copyright Basics. Washington: U.S. Government Printing Office, 1988. (Circular R1) p.3. Also includes a fuller discussion of the elements of copyright.

[2]17 U.S.C. §106 (1982). The Copyright Act of 1976, §101, begins: "Title 17 of the United States Code, entitled 'Copyright,' is hereby amended in its entirety to read as follows:..." It completely revised the Act of 1909. Therefore, the section numbers given in the text, unless otherwise noted, are to Title 17 of the United States Code (U.S.C.), 1982, as may be amended and published in its Supp.IV 1986.

[3]17 U.S.C. §202 (1982).

[4]17 U.S.C. §107-119 (1982 & Supp.IV 1986 & Pub.L.100-667, Title II, §202, Nov. 16, 1988, 102 Stat. 3949, in United States Code Congressional and Administrative News, Jan. 1989).

[5]17 U.S.C. §108(f)(1) (1982). References below to the "new Act," refer to the Copyright Act of 1976 and not to the Berne Convention Implementation Act of 1988.

[6]17 U.S.C. §107 (1982).

[7]Copyright Act of 1976, §103, Pub.L.94-553, Oct. 19, 1976, 17 U.S.C. note prec. §101 (1982).

[8]17 U.S.C. §101 (1982).

[9]17 U.S.C. §102(a) (1982).

[10]17 U.S.C. §102(b) (1982).

[11]17 U.S.C. §105 (1982).

[12]State of Georgia v. Harrison Co., 548 F.Supp. 110, 113 (N.D. Ga., Atlanta Div., 1982), case settled, order vacated, 558 F.Supp. 37 (N.D. Ga., Atlanta Div., 1983).

[13]91 F. 129, 137 (6th Cir. 1898).

[14]Pub.L.100-568, Oct. 31, 1988, eff. Mar.1, 1989. There could be a problem if copies or phonorecords were publicly distributed without notice prior to the effective date of the Berne Amendments, as the work would fall into the public domain. If no new provision to the Copyright Act of 1976 saves the copyright in such works, they could remain unprotected after the effective date of the Amendments, as §12 of the Berne Amendments "does not provide copyright protection for any work that is in the public domain in the United States."

[15]17 U.S.C. §401(b) (1982, as amended 1988, eff. Mar. 1, 1989).

[16]The same changes in notice requirements apply to phonorecords of sound recordings in 17 U.S.C. §402(a)-(b), as changed in the Berne Amendments, §7(b) (1988).

[17]17 U.S.C. §401(b)(1)-(3) (1982, as amended 1988, eff. Mar. 1, 1989).

[18]17 U.S.C. §401(c) (1982).

[19]37 C.F.R. Part 201.20 (July 1, 1988).

[20]Copyright Act of 1976, Pub.L.94-553, Oct. 19, 1976, §102, 17 U.S.C. note prec. §101 (1982).

[21]17 U.S.C. §102 and 103 (1982).

[22]17 U.S.C. §301(a) (1982).

[23]17 U.S.C. §106 (1982).

[24]17 U.S.C. §302(a) (1982).

[25]17 U.S.C. §302(b) (1982).

[26]17 U.S.C. §302(c) (1982).

[27]17 U.S.C. §303 (1982).

[28]17 U.S.C. §305 (1982).

[29]*Id.*

[30]17 U.S.C. §304(b) (1982).

[31]*Id.*

[32]"The enactments were Public Laws 87-668, 89-142, 90-141, 90-416, 91-147, 91-555, 92-170, 92-566, and 93-573. Their effect was to extend the second term of all renewed copyrights scheduled to expire between September 19, 1962 and December 31, 1976, through the end of 1976." U.S. Copyright Office. *Extension of Copyright Term in Certain Cases Under Copyright Act of 1976.* [Washington: U.S. Government Printing Office, 1985] (Circular R15t), p.2.

[33]*Id.* at p.3.

[34]17 U.S.C. §707(a) (1982). Beginning in 1979, the *Catalog* has been published on microfiche of very poor quality. It is in its Fourth Series. Renewals are volume 4, part 8, number 1 (January-June), number 2 (July-December).

[35]17 U.S.C. §101 and 102(a) (1982). U.S. Copyright Office. *Copyright Basics.* p.5.

[36]17 U.S.C. §305 (1982).

[37]U.S. Copyright Office. *Copyright Basics*, p.5.

[38]U.S. Copyright Office. *Renewal of Copyright.* [Washington: 1979] (Circular R15), p.4.

[39]The determination of death dates for works copyrighted under the new Act may be more difficult than checking on renewal registration in the 27th through 29th years from the copyright date. By 2029, the Copyright Office may have computerized a listing of death dates for registered copyright authors. See 17 U.S.C. §302(d)-(e) (1982), regarding records and presumption of author's death.

[40]17 U.S.C. §705(a)-(b) (1982). See also U.S. Copyright Office. *The Copyright Card Catalog and the Online Files of the Copyright Office.* [Washington: U.S. Government Printing Office, 1988] (Circular 23).

[41]17 U.S.C. §705(c) and §708(a)(10) (1982).

[42]U.S. Copyright Office. *How to Investigate the Copyright Status of a Work.* [Washington: 1987] (Circular R22), p.4.

SELECTED BASIC RESOURCES*

Copyright Law Reporter. Chicago: Commerce Clearing House [c1980-   ] 2 v. (loose-leaf) (Contains laws, regulations, treaties, decisions, Copyright Office circulars).

Goldstein, Paul. *Copyright: Principles, Law and Practice*. Boston: Little, Brown, 1989. 3 v.

Henn, Harry G. *Copyright Law: a Practitioner's Guide*. 2d ed. [New York] Practising Law Institute, 1988. xxix, 844 p.

The Kaminstein Legislative History Project: a Compendium and Analytical Index of Materials Leading to the Copyright Act of 1976/Alan Latman and James F. Lightstone, editors. Littleton, Colo.: Published for the Copyright Society of the U.S.A. and New York University School of Law by Fred B. Rothman & Co., 1981-1985. 6v.

Latman, Alan. *Latman's The Copyright Law*/William F. Patry. 6th ed. Washington, D.C.: Bureau of National Affairs, 1986. xviii, 687p.

Legislative History of the 1909 Copyright Act/edited and compiled by E. Fulton Brylawski and Abe Goldman. South Hackensack, N.J.: Fred B. Rothman & Co., 1976. 6 v.

Microfiche of the Documents Referred to in the Kaminstein Legislative History Project (microform) Littleton, Colo.: Fred B. Rothman & Co., 1989 (204 microfiche).

Nimmer, Melville B. and David Nimmer. *Nimmer on Copyright: a Treatise on the Law of Literacy, Musical and Artistic Property, and the Protection of Ideas*. [Albany] Matthew Bender, 1987. 4 v.

Omnibus Copyright Revision Legislative History. George S. Grossman, ed. (microform) Buffalo: Hein, c1976. 17 v. (143 microfiche).

U.S. Copyright Office. *R Circulars* (obtainable from the U.S. Copyright Office, Library of Congress, Washington, D.C. 20559. Also available for use in the U.S. depository libraries).

*No attempt has been made to make this an extensive or an exhaustive resource list or bibliography. Only a few works are noted to lead the reader to more comprehensive discussions of the copyright law. More extensive bibliographies can be found through card catalogs and database searches in libraries.

INDEX

Abbreviations 25, 27-30
    claim bases 13, 25
Annotations, *see* editorial annotations and input
Archives or libraries 3-4, 16, 82
Author or main heading 4, 11, 14, 15, 19
    death of author fn.39
    life of author plus 50 years 7, 18
    see also copyright owner
Berne Convention 6, fn.5, fn.14, fn.16
Bibliography 81
Calendar year, *see* renewals
Catalog of Copyright Entries 11-18, fn.34
    alphabetical arrangement 15-16
    cross references 12, 14, 15, 17
    date chart 31-32
    sample entry 23
Claims 4, 13
    see also abbreviations
Code of Federal Regulations (C.F.R.) 6, fn.19
Congressional acts 8-9, fn.32
    Public Law 94-553 3, fn.7, fn.20
    Public Law 100-568 fn.14
Copyright 3-14, 17-19
    claims 4
    constitutional authority 3
    duration 7-9, 18
    exclusive rights 3, 4, 7
    expiration 7-9, 12, 13, 18, fn.32
    fair use 3-4
    ideas 5
    limitations 3
    notice 3, 6, 11, 12, fn.14, fn.16
        elements 6, 13
        position 6

Copyright (*continued*)
    original date   8, 9, 12, 13, 17, 18, fn.39
    protection   3-5, 7, 9, 18, fn.14
    registration   6, 11-14, 17-19
    tangible medium of expression   4, 7
    works created   7
Copyright Act of 1909   4, 6, 7, 8, 11, 13, fn.2
Copyright Act of 1976   3-4, 6, 7-9, fn.2, fn.5, fn.7, fn.14, fn.20, fn. 32, fn. 39
    effective date   3, 8
    Public Law 94-553   3, fn.7, fn.20
Copyright Office   4, 6, 7, 11, 19, fn.1, fn.32, fn.33, fn.35, fn.37-40, fn.42
    card catalog   19
    location and address   19
    online files   19, fn.40
    search request and fee   19
Copyright owner   3, 4, 6, 7, 11, 13, 14, 17, 19
    authorize reproductions   3, 7
    distribute copies   3, 6, 7
    exclusive rights   3, 4, 7
    limitations   3
    perform or display   3, 7
    permission   6, 17
    prepare derivations   3, 7
    produce   3, 7
Court reports   5
Cross references   12, 14, 15, 17
Date chart   31-32
Duration   7-9
Editorial annotations and input   5
Exclusive rights   3-4, 7
Expiration   7-9, 12, 13, 18
Fair use   3-4
Government publications   5
Ideas   5
Laws and statutes   5
Libraries and archives   3-4, 16, 82
Library of Congress   13, 19
    main entry card in *Catalog*   13
Limitations   3
Main entry heading, *see* author or main heading

Index

Notice, *see* copyright
Original date of copyright   8, 9, 12, 13, 17, 18
Out-of-print v. out-of-copyright   9
Permission   6, 17
Photocopying   4
Protection   3-5, 7, 9, 18, fn.14
Public domain   4-5, 8, 9, 11, 13, 16, 18, fn.14
Published works   3, 4, 7, 11, 12, 13, 17, 19
Registration   4, 6, 7, 11-14, 17, 19, fn.39
Regulations   6
Renewals   7-19, fn.38
   28th year   7, 8-9, 12-13, 17-18, fn.39
   47 years   8-9, 18
   75 years   7-9, 13, 16, 18
   anniversary date   8, 9, 12, 13
   calendar year   8, 9, 12, 18
   congressional acts   8-9, fn.32
   date chart   31-32
   entry in *Catalog*   13
   extensions   8-9
   notice   14
   time limits   8, 9, 12, 17-18
Reproductions   3-4, 7
Tangible medium of expression   4, 7
Title page   6, 12
United States Code (U.S.C.)   3, fn.2-11, fn.15-18, fn.20-31, fn.34-36, fn.39-41
Unpublished works   3, 7, 17
Works made for hire   4, 7, 11